CREATED FEMALE

Cindy Bunch & Brian M. Wallace

*12 studies for
individuals or groups*

⟨ **W9-ARU-396**

CREATED MALE & FEMALE BIBLE STUDIES

*With Study Notes & Guidelines
for Leaders*

INTERVARSITY PRESS
DOWNERS GROVE, ILLINOIS 60515

The study questions in study 9 were written by Scott Hotaling.

Cover photograph: Michael Goss

Cartoon on p. 43 is taken from Church Is Stranger Than Fiction *©1990 by Mary Chambers and used by permission of InterVarsity Press.*

ISBN 0-8308-1132-X

Printed in the United States of America ∞

15	14	13	12	11	10	9	8	7	6	5	4	3	2	1
04	03	02	01	00	99	98	97	96	95	94	93			

Getting the Most out of Created Male & Female Bible Studies

Created Male and Female Bible Studies are designed to help us understand what it means to be created in the image of God. We know that God had a purpose in creating two sexes. Discovering gender distinctions is an exciting and intriguing part of what it means to be human. But sometimes it is confusing and frustrating as well. These studies will help us understand what God's purpose is for us individually and as a part of the human race.

The passages you will study will be challenging, inspiring and practical. They will show you how to think about your sexuality and how you live that out. And they will help you to better understand what the other sex is about—breaking down stereotypes and helping you find new ways to communicate.

These guides are not designed merely to convince you of the truthfulness of some idea held by the authors. Rather, they are intended to guide you into discovering biblical truths that will renew your heart and mind. How? Through an inductive approach to Bible study. Rather than simply telling you what they believe, the authors will lead you to discover what the Bible says about a particular topic through a series of questions. These studies will help you to think about the meaning of the passage so that you can truly understand what the biblical writer intended to say. Additionally, these studies are personal. At the end of each study, you'll be given an opportunity to make a commitment to respond—to take steps toward changing the way you think and act. And you'll find guidance for prayer as well.

Finally, these studies are versatile. They are designed for student, professional, neighborhood and/or church groups. They are also effective for individual study.

How They're Put Together

Created Male and Female Bible Studies have a distinctive workbook format with space for writing a response to each question. This format is ideal for personal study and allows group members to prepare in advance for the discussion or write down notes during the study. Each study takes about forty-five minutes in a group setting or thirty minutes in personal study—unless you choose to take more time.

At the end of the guide are some study notes. They do not give "the answers," but they do provide additional background information on certain questions to help you through the difficult spots. In addition, the "Guidelines for Leaders" section describes how to lead a group discussion, gives helpful tips on group dynamics and suggests ways to deal with problems which may arise during the discussion. With such helps, someone with little or no experience can lead an effective group study.

Suggestions for Individual Study

1. As you begin the study, pray that God will help you understand the passage and apply it to your life. Ask him to show you what kinds of action to take as a result of your time of study.

2. In your first session take time to read the introduction to the entire guide. This will orient you to the subject at hand and to the author's goals for the studies.

3. Read the short introduction to the study.

4. Read and reread the suggested Bible passage to familiarize yourself with it.

5. A good modern translation of the Bible will give you the most help.

The New International Version, the New American Standard Bible and the New Revised Standard Version are all recommended. The questions in this guide are based on the New International Version.

6. Use the space provided to jot your answers to the questions. This will help you express your understanding of the passage clearly.

7. Take time with the final questions and the "Respond" section in each study to commit yourself to action and/or a change in attitude. You may wish to find a study partner to discuss your insights with, one who will keep you accountable for the commitments you make.

Suggestions for Members of a Group Study

1. Come to the study prepared. Follow the suggestions for individual study mentioned above. You will find that careful preparation will greatly enrich your time spent in group discussion.

2. Be willing to participate in the discussion. The leader of your group will not be lecturing. Instead, he or she will be encouraging the members of the group to discuss what they have learned. The leader will be asking the questions that are found in this guide.

3. Stick to the topic being discussed. Your answers should be based on the verses which are the focus of the discussion.

4. Be sensitive to the other members of the group. Listen attentively when they describe what they have learned. You may be surprised by their insights! When possible, link what you say to the comments of others. Also, be affirming whenever you can. This will encourage some of the more hesitant members of the group to participate.

5. Be careful not to dominate the discussion. We are sometimes so eager to express our thoughts that we leave too little opportunity for others to respond. By all means participate! But allow others to do so as well.

6. Expect God to teach you through the passage being discussed and through the other members of the group. Pray that you will have an enjoyable and profitable time together, but also that as a result of the study you will find ways you can take action individually and/or as a group.

7. Be ready to make a personal application of the principles in the study.

The final questions will guide you in this. Although you may or may not wish to discuss the "Respond" section as a group, you may want to hold one another accountable in some way for those personal commitments. **8.** We recommend that groups agree to follow a few basic guidelines, and that these be read at the beginning of the first session. You may wish to adapt the following guidelines to your situation:

☐ Anything personal which is shared in the group is considered confidential and will not be discussed outside the group unless specific permission is given to do so.

☐ We will provide time for each person present to talk if he or she feels comfortable doing so.

☐ We will talk about ourselves and our own situations, avoiding conversation about other people.

☐ We will listen attentively to each other.

☐ We will be very cautious about giving advice.

☐ We will pray for each other.

If you are the group leader, you will find additional suggestions at the back of the guide.

How the Series Works

Where should you start? If you'd like to go through several guides in the series, whether with a group or individually, a good place to start is *Sexual Wholeness.* This guide will give you a good overview of the issues, and you may find various areas you want to explore further. While *Sexual Wholeness* may be used in either same-sex or mixed (male and female) groups, it may be uncomfortable for some in mixed groups. As a companion to that guide, you may wish to use *Created for Relationships.* If you are in a mixed group, this may be a more comfortable starting place.

Created Female and *Created Male* are designed for same-sex groups but could be used together for enlightening discussions in mixed groups. To facilitate this use, studies three through five are the same in both guides. The other studies could be intermixed so that group members have a unique opportunity to hear the perspective, needs and struggles of the other sex.

Women Facing Temptation and *Men Facing Temptation* are also designed for same-sex groups but could be adapted for use in mixed groups. You will find that all the temptations covered are applicable to either gender. This could be an opportunity for interesting discussion about how these temptations are both similar and distinct for each sex. You may discover new ways to support each other and help one another avoid temptation.

For two quarters of study on how we live out our gender roles, *Roles in Ministry* and *Following God Together* make good study companions. *Roles in Ministry* looks specifically at the role of women in the church by studying the relevant passages and is designed to help the reader find a unique place of service. Through a series of character studies involving pairs of men and women, *Following God Together* will help us see the temptations and frustrations men and women find in service together and the great possibilities for ministry when abilities are combined.

Introducing *Created Female*

I (Cindy) was recently at a major Christian conference in which a young speaker began her talk by saying, "I looked in the mirror this morning, and I thanked God for the beautiful woman he created."

How many of us would—or could—make this kind of statement in public? My first thought was to write this speaker off as prideful. Such an attitude is surely un-Christian. Then I thought, "Well, she's a minority. She has faced incredible obstacles. She had to adopt this kind of attitude to make it in her world."

But the more I pondered it, the more I appreciated the positive self-image that she exuded. This was a person who was clearly ready to be used by God. I realized it was my attitude that needed checking.

Most women struggle with issues of self-esteem. Why? To put it simply, we live in a fallen world.

One of the great sins of our culture is that we try to put people into boxes. We say such things as "Women aren't good analytical thinkers" and "Men just aren't sensitive." These labels can make us feel inferior and can limit our opportunities to use our talents.

The first study in this guide is designed to help you understand the pressures society is putting on you as a woman. It is not a Bible study as such; it sets the stage for the eleven Bible studies that follow. Study two looks at what God calls woman to be and do. Studies three through five are identical with those in *Created Male,* in case individuals or groups want to study them together. These studies set the foundation for understanding who we are in Christ.

Studies six through twelve build on the first five, looking at the qualities of a woman as outlined in Proverbs 31. In these studies we explore what it means that God has created us as women who are uniquely gifted. We will see how Christ's great love can empower us in the midst of our sin-filled world. And most of all, we will begin to understand who God wants us to be.

Have you really looked in the mirror lately? When you do, thank God for creating such an extraordinary human being. A woman.

Cindy Bunch and Brian Wallace

1
What Is a Woman?

1
Who Does My Culture Say I Am?

*W*hat's the ideal this year: thick lips or thin, large chest or small, skinny or full-bodied, long hair or short, muscular or gentle, athletic or intellectual, housewife or ad exec?

Women in Western culture cannot watch television, go to the movies or read a magazine without being told they should be something they're probably not. The advertising world is constantly using the "ideal woman" to sell its products. The problem is, the ideal seems to change constantly and, no matter what the image, few women actually measure up. Sadly, the pursuit of the ideal has led generations of women to diet, starve, exercise, study, inject fluid into their lips, suck cellulite from their thighs and insert silicone into their breasts.

<u>Whose ideal is it</u>, anyway?

Open
☐ What "feminine ideals" are you most aware of when you watch TV or read magazines?

☐ What are your feelings when you see certain women or physical traits idealized? (For instance, recently I heard someone describe Marilyn Monroe as "the essence of feminine charm and beauty.")

Study

Below are some common stereotypes of women used in advertising. Read through the descriptions and answer the questions that follow.

Cheerleader: Everyone's girl next door. Wholesome, virginal, fun and popular. She's healthy, attractive and always social.

Siren: She's beautiful, physically fit and confidently sexual—but not sleazy. She has an air of innocence, yet has perfected the playfully seductive over-the-shoulder gaze. She can be seen in beer commercials almost daily.

Ad Exec: Her gray suit and leather briefcase show that she's a successful professional. Every hair is in place, but she's not so conservative that heads don't turn. Her glasses lend an air of sophistication and intelligence. She exudes confidence; she has it all.

Buddy: Everyone's pal! Always laughing; has lots of energy. At the beach she would rather play Frisbee (though she's not necessarily good at it) than lie in the sun. She can wear the offbeat hat and get away with it. Guys may see her as really cute but not beautiful.

Debutante: Glamorous from head to toe. Epitomizes money and manners. She knows what's proper, always wears the perfect outfit. She only dates socially correct men.

Artist: Dark and mysterious. Her faraway gaze makes her seem deep in thought, profound, even troubled. She wears clothes as if her body were a canvas.

Intellectual: Often depicted in a lab coat, glasses, simple haircut and no make-up. Men usually relate to her more as a colleague than a woman. She is almost genderless in her portrayal.

Mother: In ads, she is the one who could have been a lawyer but chose to be a full-time mom instead. She is busy, dependable, intelligent in home management, never angry at the kids. Her husband thinks she's gorgeous.

Amazon: In control, powerful. Dominating. This woman is not conquered by anything. Often scantily clad and depicted as powerfully seductive. (See suntan oil ads.)

Grandmother: Her experiences can be counted by the lines in her face. She is wisdom itself. She's revered by all, feared by some.[1]

1. Of these types, which do you think men (generally speaking) . . . want to marry? *mother*

fantasize about? *siren*

remain friends with? *buddy*

take to the prom? *debutante*,

respect? *Ad Exec, grandma, intellectual*

2. Of these, which is most like you?
intellectual ? mother ?

3. Which do men see you as?

Which do other women see you as?

4. Which do you most want to be? Why?
mother, buddy, intellectual, wisdom

5. Do you ever find yourself playing the role of any of these types? In what situations and why?

6. Advertising is not the only place we hear messages about what others think we should be as women. As you were growing up, what did other women (mother, sisters, relatives, friends) tell you—verbally or nonverbally—about womanhood and femininity?

manners. "the proper way a girl should sit, stand, laugh, etc."

What were you told about womanhood by significant men in your life? (father, brothers, relatives, boyfriends)

7. What evidence from your daily living and attitudes is there that you try to conform to . . .
the "ideal" presented by advertising and media?

physique

what men or other women have told you?

what God wants you to be?

8. Why do you think many women try so hard to match the "ideal"?

9. What are two or three practical ways to avoid the trap of conforming to the world's or other people's ideals?

Respond
If appropriate, spend some time confessing to God the ways you have tried to conform to images other than the Lord's.

Identify at least one thing you can do to put more energy into becoming God's ideal woman and less energy into being the world's ideal woman.

---

[1]List adapted from Kathy Ziff, "Ads Enter New Dimensions," *Advertising Age* 56 (Sept. 12, 1985): 16-17.

2
Who Does God Want Me to Be?

Proverbs 31:10-31

A beautiful woman with a dysfunctional heart or shallow character is sort of like an elegant car whose wheels don't move. It's nothing but a shiny statue. It may look good, but it falls short of the potential for which it was created. And God created women to be much, much more than pretty statues. He created women, like men, in his own image, to reflect his character and glory.

In his camera commercial, Andre Agassi speaks for much of Western culture when he declares, "Image is everything." God says no! Beauty, femininity, godliness are found far below the surface.

Open

☐ Who are some women that you admire? Why?

☐ When people look at just your exterior image, what do they see?

Study

Read Proverbs 31:10-31 a couple of times.

1. Make a list of the things this woman does.

— make wool + linen cloth (v. 13)
— grocery shopping (14)
— cooks + directs maids (v 15)
— buys land, plants vineyard (v16)
— works late, wise (v. 17, 18)
— spins thread, weaves cloth (v 19)
— generous to needy + poor (v 20)
— makes bedspread (v. 22), cloth, belts + sells them (v 24)

2. Who are the beneficiaries of her labors?

her family

How do they benefit?

husband — leading citizen

3. What words in this passage describe the woman's character and attitudes?

— supportive   — honors the Lord
— wise   — prepares for the future
— busy, not lazy
— hardworker
— strong + industrious
— respected
— gentle

4. What does it mean to fear the Lord?

5. What character traits do you share with the woman described here?

6. In what areas do you find yourself lacking in comparison with her?

7. To what extent are you tempted to spend time developing charm and beauty (v. 30) over a noble character (v. 10) and fear of the Lord (v. 30)? Why?

8. What are one or two character traits you would like to develop?

Ask God to help you develop a simple plan of action.

Respond

God is doing a good work in you. Spend some time reflecting on those beautiful aspects of your character. Ask God to give you eyes to see what he is doing in you.

You may also want to spend some time thanking God for the ways he has graced you outwardly. Memorize Proverbs 31:30: "Charm is deceptive and beauty is fleeting; but a woman who fears the Lord is to be praised."

3
Created to Love God

Deuteronomy 6:4-9

I (Brian) found myself reading the same page over and over again. The images described caused a flood of emotion. I felt hope, joy, fear, anger and sadness all at once. Why isn't it like that for me? Could it be? I knew it was what I had always wanted.

As a college sophomore reading C. S. Lewis's *The Lion, the Witch and the Wardrobe* for the first time, I was struck by the description of how Aslan (a lion, and the Jesus figure in the book) romped and played with his friends Lucy and Susan. They were celebrating Aslan's resurrection from the dead, excited and overjoyed to see one another again. I was immediately aware of how different it was from my relationship with Jesus. I wanted to feel that kind of emotion for him. I craved a sense of anticipation and excitement at the hope of being with him in fellowship. And perhaps more than that, I longed for the sense that God wants to be with me.

That experience started me asking a question that has helped me grow more than any other: "What does it mean to love God and be loved by him?"

Open
☐ What emotions are you aware of most often?

Which emotions do you feel most comfortable expressing?

☐ How do you express your feelings of love?

☐ When do you feel most loved by God?

Study
Read Deuteronomy 6:4-9. Keep in mind that these verses follow the giving of the Ten Commandments in chapter 5.

1. How does this passage call us to love God?

2. Why are we instructed to love the Lord with all our heart and soul and strength?

3. Jesus says that this is the greatest commandment of all, and that it is this—along with the command to love our neighbors as ourselves—upon which all the Law and the Prophets hang (Matthew 22:34-40). In what ways can you see this connection?

4. Why is it important that we remember that the Lord is One?

5. What role should our love for God play in our daily lives (vv. 6-9)?

6. Suggest some visible ways and some invisible ones in which you can remind yourself (and others) about the Lord throughout the day.

7. How do you express your love for God?

8. How could you grow in loving God with every aspect of your being—all your heart, soul and strength?

9. In what practical ways do you need to let your love for God and your desire to obey him have an impact on your daily living?

Respond
In Luke 7:41-47, Jesus says that one who has been forgiven much loves much, and that one who has been forgiven little loves little. Consider that for which God has forgiven you. Respond in prayer and otherwise as God leads.

4
Created to Love God's Family

1 John 3:11-24

When people become Christians, they are plucked out of the darkness of sin and death and brought into the light of God's love and life. Standing in the light is much less like standing alone in a room under the warmth of a great lamp, and much more like standing shoulder to shoulder in God's crowded house with all the others who, like you, have been forgiven their sins. For God never calls us out of our sin and into a vacuum. He always calls us into the family of faith, where our relationship to God is to be lived out in the context of our relationship to others.

However, in our privatized Western culture, many of us spend much of our time looking for that secluded room in God's house where we can pursue our faith completely on our own. Perhaps it's because, unlike a light bulb, the light in God's house casts no shadows. It comes from every direction at once, and shines in the dark places of our hearts not usually seen. What this bright light exposes of our neighbor may appear quite ugly, and what it exposes of ourselves is usually quite embarrassing. Living in God's community can be tough, but we need to persevere—for our own spiritual health and for the sake of God's church.

Open
☐ Who are the people you regularly spend time with?

☐ In what ways do you benefit from membership in the body of Christ?

☐ What roles or responsibilities do you fill in your circle of Christian fellowship?

Study
Read 1 John 3:11-24 at least twice.
1. Make a list of the commands this passage gives.

2. How does this passage link love for the brethren and eternal life (vv. 14-16)?

3. How does this passage define love?

4. Give an example of how someone has "laid down" his or her life for you or someone you know. What were the costs?

5. What does it mean to love with words alone? Can you think of any examples?

6. Are you sometimes tempted to love with words alone? Explain.

7. What are some of the needs of the people in your church or fellowship group?

8. What are one or two specific ways you can love individuals in your fellowship with actions?

9. Do you think your participation in your church or fellowship is (a) too much, (b) too little or (c) just right? What would you like to change?

Respond
In your prayer times this week, give God thanks for the way he has used others in your life to care for you and help you grow. Ask someone to hold you accountable as you commit yourself to carrying out a specific act of love toward someone else.

5
Created to Love All People

Luke 19:1-10

*W*henever I (Brian) leave a Christian camp or conference, I invariably am filled with a desire to remain in the retreat environment year round. I think it is this same longing that causes many Christian college students to move out of their dorms and into a big house or apartment with their Christian buddies. The attraction of constant fellowship and opportunities to grow—not to mention the chance to escape some of the more negative aspects of secular college life—is powerful. Often (but not always) the results are positive. It is great to be with other believers. The love and depth of friendship can be wonderful.

But what are the costs? Who loses out? Who is not being loved?

Open

☐ In a given week, what are your regularly scheduled Christian activities?

☐ Who are the non-Christians with whom you have more than a casual acquaintance?

☐ In what settings or situations do you have significant interaction with nonbelievers? (work, school, social . . .)

Study
Read Luke 19:1-10. This may be a familiar passage to you, so be careful as you read.
1. How is Zacchaeus described in this passage?

2. What evidence is there that Zacchaeus is not well liked by the crowd in Jericho?

Why would the crowd have disliked him?

3. Compare the way Zacchaeus is treated by the crowd with the way he is treated by Jesus.

4. What is the crowd's response to Jesus' relationship with Zacchaeus?

5. Have you or folks you know ever been suspicious of someone else because of the people they hung around? Explain.

6. What are some of the reasons that you do or do not cultivate relationships with people who are not believers?

7. In what ways are you like the crowd in Jericho in your response to the "Zacchaeuses" in your community, and in what ways are you like Jesus?

8. Jesus' love brought about a transformation in Zacchaeus's life. What effect can you have on the Zacchaeuses in your community? How?

Respond
Ask God to help you develop significant relationships with people around you who need love. Consider inviting a neighbor over for dinner or a fellow worker or classmate out for a Coke. Consider praying daily for one or two people who need to come to know Jesus as Lord and Savior.

2
A Woman of Excellence

6
Strong

Judges 4:1—5:9

*T*hey were a bedraggled little family—a single missionary and her five children.

On her shoulder, Mary Slessor carried her adopted baby. Clinging to her skirt was her five year old, and with her right hand she coaxed along her three year old. Two older children sloshed behind. Sloshed, because they were trudging through a mangrove swamp in West Africa. It was night. . . . They could not see any snakes that might lie across the path or drape from trees above. But they could hear leopards. To keep the big cats at bay, Mary belted out hymns. The children chimed in.

Because no missionary had the time, or perhaps, the courage to go, Mary Slessor and her children were moving in to live with the fierce Oyokong people in what is now Nigeria. The year was 1888.[1] Such is the courage of women.

Open
☐ Name some ways you have seen women show great courage.

☐ Sometimes the courage of women is overlooked because it is different from the ways men show courage. How have you found this to be true or untrue?

Study

Read Judges 4.

1. The Israelites were repeatedly selling themselves out to idol worship. God would then turn them over to an evil king. This cycle had already taken place several times. How do these verses describe Israel at this time?

How does Deborah stand in contrast to Israel (vv. 4-7)?

2. How does Barak's response exemplify the attitude of Israel (vv. 8-9)?

3. How does Deborah show her faith and courage in verses 14-16?

4. What kind of person do you think Deborah was that Barak was given courage from her instructions?

5. How does Jael show courage and initiative in verses 17-22?

Read Judges 5:1-9.

6. Chapter 5 is Deborah's poetic retelling of the battle. What does she say about God in these verses?

7. What have Deborah and Barak learned about following God?

8. What has stepping out in faith taught you about God?

9. In what areas of your life would you like to act with greater courage?

Respond

This week find a creative way to affirm a woman you know who has demonstrated great courage.

---

[1]Miriam Adeney, *A Time for Risking* (Portland, Ore.: Multnomah, 1987), pp. 147-48.

7
Trustworthy

Luke 16:1-15

Matt 25:14-30

What *has* God entrusted to you? How do we make it multiply for God?
— identify what they are.

*B*eing trustworthy is a quality that sounds dated. The word almost sounds quaint to our modern ears. Yet it is a quality that Christ focused on when he taught his disciples.

In Christ's parable being trustworthy is more than just avoiding negative behaviors like stealing, lying and cheating. Being trustworthy involves active behaviors. We must make the most of what we are given, putting our unique abilities to good use.

Open
☐ What does it mean to be trustworthy?

☐ What are the qualities of a trustworthy person?

Study
Read Luke 16:1-15. (parable of shrewd Manager)

1. What key words highlight the main topics in this passage?

2. Why was the manager going to be fired (vv. 1-2)?

3. Describe the action the manager took (vv. 3-7).

4. What benefit did the manager expect to receive from his actions (vv. 3-4)?

5. Why did the master commend the manager (vv. 8-9)?

6. From this passage explain the difference between being "dishonest" and being "shrewd."

7. What are the principles Jesus is highlighting in verses 10-13?

8. How do Jesus' teachings relate to the story he told?

9. In what ways do the values of the world (v. 5) make it difficult to be a trustworthy person?

Respond

Begin to analyze your own motives at work and in relationships with others. Are you being a shrewd manager of the resources you have been given? Or are you being dishonest with yourself and others for the sake of your own interests?

8
Wise

Ephesians 1:3-23

*M*ama says, 'Don't start nothing. But if *they* start something, don't come in here cryin'. Finish it.' "

This down-to-earth advice is an example conference speaker Toinette Eugene gave in describing her mother's wisdom. Mama had many original sayings which she used to encourage and teach her children.

Our culture is filled with signs of the wisdom of women. This study will be an opportunity to celebrate that fact—and to reflect on how we gain true wisdom.

Open
The following are words of wisdom from some fairly well-known women:
"A bird doesn't sing because he has an answer—he sings because he has a song."—Jean Anglund
"Real success is willingness to accept God's place for us today."—Ann Kiemel
"God don't always come when you think he should, but he's always on time."—Alex Haley, quoting his grandmother

"The ghosts of things that never happened are worse than the ghosts of things that did."—L. M. Montgomery, author of *Anne of Green Gables,* in *Emily's Quest*

"To be a close follower of Jesus was to learn not to ask, 'Exactly what will it be like?' but to ask rather, 'What must I do to be ready for it?' "—Monica Hellwig, theologian

☐ Which of these do you consider wise sayings, from your own beliefs and experience? Explain.

☐ What quotes from women you know would you add to this list?

Study

Read Ephesians 1:3-14.

1. List everything verses 4-5 tell you about how God created us.

2. What has God given us in Jesus Christ (vv. 6-10)?

3. What has God given us in the Holy Spirit (vv. 13-14)?

4. Why has God given us so much (v. 12)?

Read Ephesians 1:15-23.

5. What gifts is Paul asking God to grant to the Ephesians?

Why do we need each of these gifts today?

6. Why do you think Paul prays specifically for "the Spirit of wisdom and revelation" for them?

7. What does it mean to have "the eyes of your heart enlightened" (v. 18)?

8. God's power (described in vv. 19-23) is available to *you.* How does knowing this make you feel?

9. As a woman, in what area do you have a unique ability or opportunity to offer wisdom?

Respond
Make a commitment to do something which will help you to grow in your wisdom and knowledge about Christ. It could be reading a particular book, joining a Sunday-school class, making a commitment to pray with someone, learning more about meditating on Scripture, fasting or anything else you feel a spiritual hunger to learn about.

9
Resourceful

1 Samuel 25:1-42

*Q*uilters is a musical which depicts the life of early western settlers from a female perspective. In the play an elderly mother makes her daughters a quilt in which each block represents an aspect of her life. She tells stories of desperately piecing scraps late into the cold nights to ensure that her family has adequate warm covering. She describes the community events of gathering to make quilts for others who are in need. Finally, she describes beautiful festive quilts made in honor of the times of celebration in her life.

Quilts are just one example of the resourcefulness and creativity our foremothers modeled for us. In this study we will meet a godly woman who used her own ingenuity to save her family.

Open
☐ Give an example of resourcefulness from recent national or international events.

☐ Give an example of how a woman you know is resourceful.

Study
Read 1 Samuel 25:1-42.
1. What request does David make of Abigail's husband, Nabal (vv. 7-8)?

2. What is Nabal's response?

3. What is the situation when the servant comes to Abigail to ask for her intervention?

4. Why do you think the servant decided to talk to Abigail?

5. What is your impression of Abigail from her actions in this passage?

6. What are the important elements of Abigail's actions in vv. 18-31?

7. Who were the beneficiaries of Abigail's resourceful actions, and how did they benefit?

8. What internal and external resources has God given you to enable you to serve others?

How can you better use them?

Respond
Whether it is a commitment on a large or small scale, find a way to put your response to question 8 into action.

10
Beautiful

1 Peter 3:1-7

*B*eauty is as beauty does."

You've probably heard that old saying at some point in your life. And it probably didn't help you feel any better about yourself. At the same time, the models of the perfect woman that the world holds up set such an impossible standard that they only bring frustration.

The following passage will help you to consider what constitutes inner and outer beauty in God's eyes.

Solomon tells me I'm one in a thousand!

Open

☐ What are some ways the world defines beauty?

☐ How can the desire to measure up to worldly definitions of beauty be used to control or manipulate women (as shown in the cartoon on the previous page)?

☐ When do you feel beautiful?

Study

Read 1 Peter 3:1-7.

1. What are the characteristics of a holy woman according to this passage?

2. What does it mean to be "submissive" as it is described here (vv. 1-2, 5-6)?

How would this make a person beautiful?

3. How do verses 3-4 define beauty?

4. In what ways is this compatible with the world's definition?

How is it incompatible?

5. In what ways is Sarah a role model we should emulate? (Draw from both vv. 5-6 and your knowledge of Sarah in the Old Testament.)

6. Verse 7 describes a husband's response. How does this response flow from the wife's godliness?

7. When have you been surprised and/or pleased to see the world recognize a godly woman?

8. In what way(s) does your attitude about beauty need to change?

Respond
As you go about each day's activities this week, notice the messages about beauty around you (on billboards, in stores, in magazines). Ask God to free you of worldly ideas of beauty so you can discover what godly beauty is.

11
Content

Philippians 4:10-20

*I*f I only had . . ."

How would you fill in the blank? Would it be "a little more money," "a boyfriend," "a day off" or "a new car"? Sometimes we think that contentment is just around the corner. If we could only have this one elusive thing, our lives would be complete.

But it never happens.

In his letter to the Philippians Paul writes of a much richer contentment.

Open
☐ What "one thing" do you sometimes find yourself thinking would bring you contentment?

☐ How has that "one thing" changed in the course of your life?

☐ Why do you think that is?

Study
Read Philippians 4:10-20.
1. From this passage, how would you describe the tone of the letter?

2. What has the Philippian church done for Paul?

3. In verses 11 and 17-18 Paul emphasizes that he isn't asking for further gifts. Why do you think this is?

4. What does Paul mean when he says that he has learned "the secret of being content" (vv. 11-13)?

5. How is the strength of Christ an encouragement to you when you feel discontented?

6. What do you learn about Paul from verses 15-16?

7. How has verse 19 been real for you?

8. What do you need to learn from Paul's example here?

Respond

Do not let a day go by this week without thanking God for one gift each day brings. Even if it is difficult for you to really feel the thankfulness at first, persist in prayer. Eventually, the feelings will follow your actions.

12
Confident

Hebrews 10:19-25, 32-36

Women write autobiographies very differently from men. Even when they have been very successful, they apologize for their weaknesses and try to explain them—rather than focusing on the positives.[1]

This is a telling fact. And it is one of many clues which suggest that women often sin not by being overconfident but by being underconfident. We may think that we are being humble and righteous. In reality we are unwilling or unable to trust ourselves. In the process, we reveal our lack of trust in God as well.

Open

☐ What movie or TV character exemplifies confidence for you? Why?

☐ When is it easy for you to express confidence in yourself?

When is it hard?

Study
Read Hebrews 10:19-25.
1. How do these verses tell us that we can be close to God?

2. Why would the original readers of this letter have experienced this as a great privilege (vv. 19-21)?

3. What does verse 22 tell us is required in order to draw near to God?

4. Describe a person you know who holds "unswervingly" to faith.

5. How does the body of Christ give us confidence (vv. 24-25)? (Respond from the text and give examples from your own experience.)

Read Hebrews 10:32-36.
6. What situation is described in verses 32-34?

How did they encourage each other to maintain faith?

7. In what ways would it be difficult for a woman with low self-confidence to maintain faith in God?

8. When are you tempted to "throw away your confidence"?

9. What enables you to maintain confidence in Christ?

Respond
Consider what your own level of confidence is like. To what extent do you allow lack of confidence to keep you from serving God? Confess your difficulties to God. Ask him to give you strength and faith that you might use the gifts you have been given to their fullest.

---

[1]Carolyn Heilbrun, *Writing a Woman's Life* (New York: Norton, 1988), pp. 22, quoted in Mary Ellen Ashcroft, *Temptations Women Face* (Downers Grove, Ill.: InterVarsity Press, 1991), p. 29.

Guidelines for Leaders

Leading a Bible discussion can be an enjoyable and rewarding experience. But it can also be intimidating—especially if you've never done it before. If this is how you feel, you're in good company.

Remember when God asked Moses to lead the Israelites out of Egypt? Moses replied, "O Lord, please send someone else to do it" (Exodus 4:13). But God gave Moses the help (human and divine) he needed to be a strong leader.

Leading a Bible discussion is not difficult if you follow certain guidelines. You don't need to be an expert on the Bible or a trained teacher. The suggestions listed below can help you to effectively fulfill your role as leader—and enjoy doing it.

Preparing for the Study

1. As you study the passage ahead of time, ask God to help you understand it and apply it in your own life. Unless this happens, you will not be prepared to lead others. Pray too for the various members of the group. Ask God to open your hearts to the message of his Word and motivate you to action.

2. Read the introduction to the entire guide to get an overview of the subject at hand and the issues which will be explored.

3. Be ready for the "Open" questions with a personal story or example.

The group will be only as vulnerable and open as its leader.

4. As you begin preparing for each study, read and reread the assigned Bible passage to familiarize yourself with it.

5. This study guide is based on the New International Version of the Bible. It will help you and the group if you use this translation as the basis for your study and discussion.

6. Carefully work through each question in the study. Spend time in meditation and reflection as you consider how to respond.

7. Write your thoughts and responses in the space provided in the study guide. This will help you to express your understanding of the passage clearly.

8. It might help you to have a Bible dictionary handy. Use it to look up any unfamiliar words, names or places. (For additional help on how to study a passage, see chapter five of *Leading Bible Discussions,* IVP.)

9. Take the final (application) questions and the "Respond" portion of each study seriously. Consider what this means for your life—what changes you may need to make in your lifestyle and/or actions you can take in your church or with people you know. Remember that the group will follow your lead in responding to the studies.

Leading the Study

1. Be sure everyone in your group has a study guide and Bible. Encourage the group to prepare beforehand for each discussion by reading the introduction to the guide and by working through the questions in the study.

2. At the beginning of your first time together, explain that these studies are meant to be discussions, not lectures. Encourage the members of the group to participate. However, do not put pressure on those who may be hesitant to speak during the first few sessions.

3. Begin the study on time. Open with prayer, asking God to help the group understand and apply the passage.

4. Have a group member read the introductory paragraph at the beginning of the discussion. This will remind the group of the topic of the study.

5. Every study begins with a section called "Open." These "approach" questions are meant to be asked before the passage is read. They are important for several reasons.

First, there is always a stiffness that needs to be overcome before people will begin to talk openly. A good question will break the ice.

Second, most people will have lots of different things going on in their minds (dinner, an exam, an important meeting coming up, how to get the car fixed) that have nothing to do with the study. A creative question will get their attention and draw them into the discussion.

Third, approach questions can reveal where our thoughts or feelings need to be transformed by Scripture. That is why it is especially important not to read the passage before the approach question is asked. The passage will tend to color the honest reactions people would otherwise give, because they feel they are supposed to think the way the Bible does.

6. Have a group member read aloud the passage to be studied.

7. As you ask the questions, keep in mind that they are designed to be used just as they are written. You may simply read them aloud. Or you may prefer to express them in your own words.

There may be times when it is appropriate to deviate from the study guide. For example, a question may already have been answered. If so, move on to the next question. Or someone may raise an important question not covered in the guide. Take time to discuss it, but try to keep the group from going off on tangents.

8. Avoid answering your own questions. Repeat or rephrase them if necessary until they are clearly understood. An eager group quickly becomes passive and silent if members think the leader will give all the "right" answers.

9. Don't be afraid of silence. People may need time to think about the question before formulating their answers.

10. Don't be content with just one answer. Ask "What do the rest of you think?" or "Anything else?" until several people have given answers to a question.

11. Acknowledge all contributions. Be affirming whenever possible. Never reject an answer. If it is clearly off base, ask "Which verse led you to that conclusion?" or "What do the rest of you think?"

12. Don't expect every answer to be addressed to you, even though this will probably happen at first. As group members become more at ease, they will begin to truly interact with each other. This is one sign of healthy discussion.

13. Don't be afraid of controversy. It can be stimulating! If you don't resolve an issue completely, don't be frustrated. Move on and keep it in mind for later. A subsequent study may solve the problem.

14. Periodically summarize what the group has said about the passage. This helps to draw together the various ideas mentioned and gives continuity to the study. But don't preach.

15. Don't skip over the application questions at the end of each study. It's important that we each apply the message of the passage to ourselves in a specific way. Be willing to get things started by describing how you have been affected by the study.

Depending on the makeup of your group and the length of time you've been together, you may or may not want to discuss the "Respond" section. If not, allow the group to read it and reflect on it silently. Encourage members to make specific commitments and to write them in their study guide. Ask them the following week how they did with their commitments.

16. Conclude your time together with conversational prayer. Ask for God's help in following through on the commitments you've made.

17. End on time.

Many more suggestions and helps are found in *The Big Book on Small Groups, Small Group Leaders' Handbook* and *Good Things Come in Small Groups* (IVP). Reading through one of these books would be worth your time.

Study Notes

Study 1. Who Does My Culture Say I Am?

Purpose: To identify some of the common stereotypes of women in Western culture and how they have affected our lifestyles and attitudes.

General note. This is not a Bible study but a tool to foster discussion and individual awareness. Encourage the group to be as honest as they can about their emotions. When confronted with these stereotypes, women may feel angry, hurt, belittled, boxed in, confused or inadequate. The point of this exercise is to get in touch with those emotions as well as understand where the pressures are coming from. Encourage one another to be honest about how—knowingly or not—you may be giving in to cultural pressure. (See question 8 specifically.)

Remember that many of the questions ask for generalities. There are no right or wrong answers. Speak for yourself from your own experience, and help others do the same.

Study 2. Who Does God Want Me to Be? Proverbs 31:10-31.

Purpose: To show what God wants women to be.

General note. An interesting literary device is used here: the NIV points out that verses 10-31 form an acrostic, each verse beginning with a successive letter of the Hebrew alphabet.

It is tempting to read this passage as a list of things to do, which may lead to frustration and discouragement. It may be more helpful to emphasize, as the questions try to do, issues of being rather than doing.

Think about what God wants you to *be*, with regard to your character and attitudes.

Question 2. Not only her children and husband, but her servants and the needy. Ultimately even she herself benefits.

Question 3. We are asking what character traits her actions demonstrate. Eager for work (v. 13), thoughtful (v. 16), charitable (v. 20), hopeful for the future (v. 25), wise (v. 26), faithful (v. 26), not idle (v. 27).

Question 4. The fear of the Lord includes not only a healthy respect and reverence, but an awareness of God's power and position that brings humility and obedience.

Question 7. Remember that charm and beauty are not in themselves sinful, but they are not to be desired and pursued before godliness. Therefore, what may be a sinful act for one person may not be for all. (Going to the spa or dieting is normal for most, but when it becomes a compulsive behavior it may signal an unhealthy overemphasis on the physical.)

Study 3. Created to Love God. Deuteronomy 6:4-9.

Purpose: To show that, whether we are created male or female, we are all created by God, for a love relationship with God.

Question 1. These verses call us to love God and express that love in obedience to his commands. This may be freeing for members of the group who are less emotional—and who may wonder if they are less spiritual because they feel less emotion for the Lord. You may want to follow up this question by asking, "What role does emotion play in our love for the Lord?"

Question 2. God desires our love for him to be all-inclusive. We should love him with all our being: not just our emotions, but our minds (the way we think) and bodies (the way we act) as well.

Question 4. For the Israelites, it was a helpful reminder that, unlike the peoples around them who had numerous gods, they had but one object of their devotion, the Lord. We too must be careful not to let our hearts wander.

Questions 5-6. The exhortations in verses 6-9 are helpful means of never letting the Lord stray from our hearts and minds. Note that these are not necessarily commands to be followed literally.

Question 7. Encourage the group that there is no one way that we should express love for God. As individuals we are all different. Some may be more intellectual, others emotional. However, obedience to the Lord is universal. If we love God we will obey God.

Study 4. Created to Love God's Family. 1 John 3:11-24.

Purpose: To explore how, as children of God, we are all called to love others in the family of faith, God's church.

Question 2. Our love for our Christian brothers and sisters provides us assurance of our salvation—it is a sign that we have passed from death to life.

Question 3. See verse 16. Jesus' death on our behalf is the ultimate example of love for others.

Question 4. Use this question to explore what "laying down our lives for others" means practically.

Questions 7-9. Use these questions to prompt discussion about your particular fellowship or church. Is there a healthy commitment or are members disconnected? What can be done?

Respond. As the group leader, it may be appropriate for you to ask members not currently in fellowship to respond to the study by making some decisions concerning their participation in the body of Christ.

Study 5. Created to Love All People. Luke 19:1-10.

Purpose: To understand and act on God's call for us to love all people.

Questions 1-2. In verse 3 we are told that Zacchaeus wanted to see Jesus but was short and could not because of the crowd. He obviously could not see over them, and it seems the crowd would not let him through to stand in front of them. In verse 7, they call him *a sinner,* one known to break God's law. It was common—even expected—that righteous people would not associate with such as Zacchaeus. Being a tax collector, he made his living taking money from his own people on behalf of the hated Roman occupation. Tax collectors were considered to be traitors. Further, individuals in the crowd may have had personal reasons to dislike Zacchaeus; the fact that he was wealthy and the chief tax collector tells us that he was probably adept at overcharging people to his own benefit.

Question 5. Sometimes people question why a Christian would join a fraternity or participate in a secular community-service organization. The Christian is made to feel less spiritual for spending time outside of "Christian" activities. This is the classic "guilty by association" charge.

Question 7. Think about common attitudes toward not only the folks who are known "sinners" (carousers, drunkards, adulterers), but also those with AIDS, the homeless, those struggling with homosexuality, recent immigrants, people with disabilities and so on.

Question 8. Just a little expression of love and acceptance can have a powerful effect on a person's life. Jesus' love for Zacchaeus prompted a genuine repentance.

Study 6. Strong. Judges 4:1—5:9.

Purpose: To discover what it means to be a woman of strength who can influence and inspire people to God's glory.

Question 1. Read Judges 3:12-31 for the background of Israel's pattern of disobedience. Ehud was God's deliverer from an evil king. God had given Israel over to the king after they disobeyed. Deborah was a prophetess and thus was called to speak the word from God, in this case to Barak.

Question 2. Verse 9 tells us that Barak was acting cowardly because he didn't trust God.

Question 3. Deborah trusts in the Lord's command despite Barak's doubt. She reminds Barak that the king heads up the army (see, for example, 1 Samuel 8:20). This spurs him to action.

Question 4. It is clear that she possessed the strength of God and spoke with the authority of God. For Barak the advantage of having a prophetess along would be the sense that God's presence in the battle would be more real, and both troops and leaders would be more optimistic.

Question 5. Jael seems to be working on her own. She has devised a way to get Sisera into the tent. She carries out her plan quickly and effectively.

Question 6. Remembering a victory in song was a traditional practice (see, for example, Exodus 15:1-18). Verses 4-5 refer to the Lord's appearance in a storm cloud to lead Israel into Canaan (see Exodus 13:21).

Study 7. Trustworthy. Luke 16:1-15.

Purpose: To consider what it means to be a woman in whom others can put their trust.

Question 1. Note the words "master" (v. 3), "dishonest" (v. 8), "shrewd" (v. 8), "worldly" (v. 9), "wealth (v. 9), "trustworthy" (v. 11) and "servant" (v. 13).

Question 2. Apparently the manager was being wasteful and neglectful of his master's business (v. 1). In verse 8 he is also called "dishonest."

Question 3. The master may have been overcharging the debtors because the Mosaic law didn't allow him to charge interest. Thus, the manager may have simply returned the debts to their original amounts and satisfied both the master and the debtors. Or the manager may have been cheating his master by not collecting what was owed to him. Either way, the manager was wisely planning his own future (*The NIV Study Bible*, Kenneth L. Barker, gen. ed. [Grand Rapids, Mich.: Zondervan, 1985], p. 1571).

Question 4. Knowing that he was going to be out of work, the manager planned for the future by lowering the debts of those who owed his master money. This caused the debtors to be obligated to him.

Question 6. In this passage Jesus equates shrewdness with careful planning and skillful deal making. Dishonesty is equated with wastefulness and neglect (v. 1).

Question 8. In verse 9 Jesus points out that the one way for the steward to ensure that he has a heavenly home is to begin using resources well in his daily life. "Worldly wealth" refers not only to money, but to all the things of this world. "Although these things—your property, ability, time—belong to this life only, says Jesus, yet what will happen to you then, when you pass into that [eternal] life, will depend on what you are doing with them here and now. Make sure that your use of them brings you into a fellowship of friends which will survive beyond death" (Michael Wilcock, *The Message of Luke* [Downers Grove, Ill.: InterVarsity Press, 1979], p. 160).

Study 8. Wise. Ephesians 1:3-23.
Purpose: To explore the depth and power of true wisdom.
Question 1. We were chosen before our creation, have been made holy and blameless and are made his children through Jesus Christ.
Question 5. He asks for "the Spirit of wisdom and revelation" (v. 17), that the "eyes" of their hearts would be "enlightened" and that they would know the hope to which God has called them, the "riches of his glorious inheritance" (v. 18) and his great power (v. 19).
Question 7. The literal reference would be to the mind or inner discernment and understanding. Move beyond that to consider the implications of such understanding.

Study 9. Resourceful. 1 Samuel 25:1-42.
Purpose: To consider how a woman's ingenuity can help and protect those around her.
Question 1. David is asking for a reward for his protection of Nabal's men when they were in his territory. According to the Word Biblical Commentary, "His ten-person delegation . . . carried out a detailed and respectful protocol. David addressed Nabal as 'my brother' . . . wishing peace to the man himself, to his whole household, and to everything he had. The narrator wants us to understand that David sought neither to harm Nabal and his family nor to diminish him in any way of his lavish holdings. . . . David's self-designation as son displayed reverence and respect" (Ralph W. Klein, *1 Samuel,* David Hubbard, gen. ed. [Waco, Tex.: Word, 1983], p. 248).
Question 5. Abigail acted quickly and wisely. Her words were carefully chosen and persuasive. This action kept David from the shame of fighting a fool (ibid., p. 249), from shedding blood and from overstepping his bounds to gain victory. These latter two would have been a discredit to his royal character. "Whereas David boldly refused the opportunity to kill Saul in chapters 25 and 26, only the action of Abigail prevents him from blood guilt in the case of Nabal" (ibid., p. 251).
Question 6. She worked quickly (v. 18); she personally rode to meet David (v. 20); she showed humility before David (v. 23); she accepted

the blame for what had happened (v. 24); she asked for God's blessings on David (vv. 26, 28-31).

Study 10. Beautiful. 1 Peter 3:1-7.

Purpose: To discover what true beauty is and how we can develop it.

Question 1. A holy woman is described as "submissive" and able to win over an unbeliever by her words and actions (v. 1). She has "purity" and "reverence" (v. 2). She is not showy or ostentatious (v. 3). Her beauty comes from the inside, reflecting a "gentle and quiet spirit" (v. 4).

Question 2. Submission here does not refer to a lower status or inferiority. Rather, the passage as a whole seems to suggest a gracious attitude which is concerned with the needs of others. Some may interpret this as a reference to the principle of headship as it is described in Ephesians 5:22-33. Others may focus on Ephesians 5:21, which commands all believers to submit to one another "out of reverence for Christ."

Question 5. For background on Sarah see Genesis 12:10-20 and 18:1-15.

Question 6. See also Ephesians 5:25-33 for the husband's responsibilities.

Study 11. Content. Philippians 4:10-20.

Purpose: To explore what contentment is like and what the source of it is.

Question 1. Notice the words that indicate Paul's joy: in verse 10, "rejoice" and in verses 11 and 12, "content." He expresses confidence in Christ's provision in verses 11-13. He expresses gratefulness for the help he received from the Philippians and goodwill toward them (vv. 14-19).

Question 2. In verse 15 Paul says that at the beginning of his ministry in that area, the Philippians were the only ones giving to him. They continued supporting him even when he left the area (v. 16). They have recently sent gifts (vv. 10, 18).

Question 3. It may be suggested that Paul is actually asking for gifts—in a roundabout way. The tone of the letter, however, seems

sincerely grateful. Don't let disagreement over this throw you off track.
Question 4. The focus on Christ's provision in verse 13 should lead
you to a response.
Question 6. Paul is not bitter although he was wronged by the church.
He focuses on the positive side—the gifts that were given. Skip this
question if it is covered in question 2.
Question 7. Discuss concrete ways and actual situations in which you
have experienced God meeting your needs.

Study 12. Confident. Hebrews 10:19-25, 32-36.
Purpose: To find confidence in God and in ourselves through faith.
Question 1. This passage tells us we can be close to God through Jesus'
blood (vv. 19-20) and by drawing near to God in faith (v. 22).
Question 2. Verse 20 refers to the curtain in the temple which
separated the Holy Place from the Most Holy Place—where only the
high priest was allowed (Exodus 26:31-33). When Christ died, it was
ripped in two (Mark 15:38), signifying that all people were now able to
enter God's presence.
   Verse 21 refers to Jesus as a priest. He intervenes with God on our
behalf as a priest according to Old Testament law. As noted above, in
the temple the priests had certain privileges such as entering the Holy
Place to be in God's presence. Through Christ's blood, we are all given
equal opportunity to approach God and communicate with him.
Question 3. Four factors are required to approach God: (1) a sincere
heart, (2) full assurance of faith, (3) freedom from a guilty conscience
and (4) bodies washed with pure water.
   This last requirement refers not to an "external ceremony such as
baptism but a figure for inner cleansing, of which the washing of the
priests under the old covenant was a symbol (see Ex 30:19-21; Lev
8:6)" (*The NIV Study Bible,* p. 1871).
Question 5. Verses 24-25 tell us to encourage each other to love and
good works. Take time to consider what this looks like on a practical
level.